Literary Newsmakers for Students, Volume 2

Project Editor: Anne Marie Hacht

Editorial: Ira Mark Milne

Rights Acquisition and Management: Margaret Chamberlain-Gaston and Robyn Young Manufacturing: Rita Wimberly

Imaging: Lezlie Light, Mike Logusz, and Kelly Quin Product Design: Pamela A. E. Galbreath Vendor Administration: Civie Green

Product Manager: Meggin Condino

© 2006 Gale, a part of Cengage Learning Inc.

Cengage and Burst Logo are trademarks and Gale is a registered trademark used herein under license.

For more information, contact
Gale, an imprint of Cengage Learning
27500 Drake Rd.
Farmington Hills, MI 48331-3535
Or you can visit our Internet site at

of the publisher and verified to the satisfaction of the publisher will be corrected in future editions.

ISBN 13: 978-1-4144-0282-6
ISBN 10: 1-4144-0282-1
ISSN: 1559-9639

This title is also available as an e-book
ISBN-13: 978-1-4144-2930-4, ISBN-10: 1-4144-2930-4
Contact your Gale, an imprint of Cengage Learning representative for ordering information.

Printed in the United States of America
10 9 8 7 6 5 4 3 2 1

The Time Traveler's Wife

Audrey Niffenegger

2004

Introduction

The Time Traveler's Wife is Audrey Niffenegger's first novel. Though twenty-five agents initially turned down the manuscript, the book ventured on to great success, selling over a million copies in both the United States and the United Kingdom. The debut novel has garnered several awards, including the British Book Award of 2006, and has reached the *New York Times* bestseller list, among others. Actors Brad Pitt and Jennifer Aniston started a bidding war among potential publishers by securing the film rights to the novel for their production company, Plan B, in 2003, before the book was published.

The Time Traveler's Wife chronicles the romance between Henry, a Chicago librarian who vanishes in and out of time, and Clare, an artist who first encounters him as a child. Despite its science-fiction premise, the novel is more about the love and longing, the joy and melancholy, between star-crossed soul mates. Niffenegger says the story was inspired by the love between her maternal grandparents. Her grandfather died young, and her grandmother, who lived another three decades, never remarried. As she explains in her biography on the website *BookBrowse*, "I wanted to write about a perfect marriage that is tested by something outside the control of the couple."

The resulting novel has charmed readers around the world and provided countless book clubs with fuel for passionate discussion. Judith Mass captured its appeal in her 2003 review for the *Boston Globe*: "Refreshingly, the novel portrays long-term commitment as something lively and exuberant rather than dutiful and staid, evoking both the comforts it brings us and the tribulations we learn to live with."

Author Biography

Born June 13, 1963, Audrey Niffenegger spent her childhood writing and imagining in Evanston, Illinois. She earned her bachelor of fine arts degree from the School of the Art Institute of Chicago in 1985 and her master of fine arts from Northwestern University in 1991. While writing *The Time Traveler's Wife*, Niffenegger lived in Chicago and taught writing, letterpress printing, and fine edition book production at the Interdisciplinary Book Arts MFA Program at the Columbia College Chicago Center for Book and Paper Arts. Her fiction has been published in *Bust, The Magnetic Poetry Book of Poetry*, and *Electronic Book Review*, while her visual art can be found in the collections of the Newberry Library, the National Museum of Women in the Arts, the Library of Congress, the Houghton Library at Harvard University, and Temple University, among others.

In writing *The Time Traveler's Wife*, Niffenegger received several fellowships including a Ragdale Foundation Fellowship received nine years in a row, as well as a Fellowship in Prose from the Illinois Arts Council in 2000 and an Artist's Grant from the Ludwig Vogelstein Foundation in 1991.

In 2005, Niffenegger published *Three Incestuous Sisters: An Illustrated Novel*, a tragic, erotic, and Gothic tale about three sisters who love the same man. Another illustrated novel, *The Adventuress*, is expected in 2006. Niffenegger's creative inspiration comes from an eclectic variety of artistic sources, including Aubrey Beardsley, Max Klinger, Edvard Munch, Japanese prints, and silent films such as *Nosferatu* and *The Cabinet of Dr. Caligari*. As of 2006, Niffenegger lives in Chicago and continues to write and create visual art.

Prologue

The Time Traveler's Wife opens with two people each describing how they feel about being separated from their partner. Clare Abshire waits for a man who may never revisit her life, while Henry DeTamble describes his complex emotions about jumping unexpectedly through time: confusion, euphoria, desire, fear, and anxiety.

Part One: The Man Out of Time

Chapter 1: First Date, One

In October 1991, when Henry is twenty-eight and Clare is twenty, Clare visits the Newberry Library to research paper making techniques and sees Henry, the man she has loved since childhood. But because of Henry's time travel, he does not recognize her; in his experience, they have not yet met. This is their first meeting with both of them in the "present." Joyful, Clare asks him on a date. Though Henry is bewildered by her familiar attitude, he accepts.

Later that evening during their date, Henry asks Clare to tell him everything she knows about their relationship. Clare shows him a sixteen-page list of dates they had met from September 23, 1977, to May 24, 1989. She briefly recaps their rendezvous over the years, as well as details about herself. She is from a wealthy family, and she is studying at the Art Institute. Henry tells Clare about his parents, details the "older Henry" had never provided, such as his surname and profession. She realizes that, although she has known him since childhood, he has never met her. After dinner, impassioned by the arrival of their future, they make love. The next morning, Clare is startled to find a woman's belongings in Henry's bathroom. She is not angry that he has dated other women because he had not known she was coming. Clare and Henry continue to revel in their connection.

Chapter 2: A First Time for Everything

Henry recalls his fifth birthday, June 16, 1968, when his parents, both professional musicians, took him to the Field Museum of Natural History. The museum enchanted him, seeming to freeze both nature and time. The day ends with both dinner at Mr. and Mrs. Kim's (he calls her Kimy), the landlords who lived downstairs, and Henry's first time-traveling experience. The five-year-old Henry finds himself at the museum "a little earlier in the evening," where he is greeted by a twenty-four-year-old Henry, who explains time travel to him.

Chapter 3: First Date, Two

Clare meets Henry for the first time on September 23, 1977, when she is six and he is thirty-six, in the meadow behind her Michigan home, the Meadowlark House. Suspicious of the man standing naked in the Meadow, she grills him for personal information. Henry reveals he is a time traveler and has met her before, or rather after. On a piece of paper, he writes down the next date when they will meet and disappears. Henry travels from the day Clare first met him to 2000, a time when they are together as a couple. Then, six days after their first meeting in September 1977, Henry reappears in the Meadow as promised, where an anxious Clare gives him some of her father's clothing. Henry tries to explain time traveling and says he will return on October 16.

Chapter 4: Lessons in Survival

In June 1973, a twenty-seven-year-old Henry and a nine-year-old Henry visit the Art Institute of Chicago. The elder Henry teaches the younger how to survive the unpredictable and inconvenient nature of time travel; since he arrives in each time and place without clothing or money, he must learn skills to protect himself. Though young Henry is wary and nervous at first, he follows the advice and pickpockets a wallet. After the lessons, the elder Henry informs the younger that they are the same person. Young Henry feels sad that there is no one like him. In December 1978, a future Henry fails to prevent an embarrassing moment for a present Henry. Elder Henry explains he does not have the power to change outcomes because events and experiences have already occurred. Four years later, in 1982, nineteen-year-old Henry has been arrested for breaking and entering. Henry is wanted by the police for a series of minor crimes, all committed to survive his unexpected traveling. As usual, he vanishes before the police can arrest him.

In April 1984, Henry and Clare play in the Meadow. The thirty-six-year-old Henry becomes jealous of her girlish crush on Paul McCartney while Clare is disappointed to hear Henry is married. Henry does not reveal that she is his wife. The following year, Clare bristles when Henry tells her things about her future self, unhappy with the notion that the future is already determined. Henry struggles with his desire for this girl who will be his wife.

Chapter 5: After the End

In 1984, Clare has a confusing moment when she sees Henry with her father and brother, who are hunting in the Meadow. In February 1987, fifteen-year-old Clare and thirty-eight-year-old Henry meet in the Reading Room, a room in Meadowlark House that Clare fixed especially for him. Henry accidentally speaks of Clare's mother, Lucille, in the past tense, and he is forced to tell her how her mother will die.

In June 1987, at sixteen years old, Clare invites thirty-two-year-old Henry to her friend Ruth's birthday party. Clare's friend Helen confronts him and accuses him of being Clare's secret boyfriend, which he denies. After a traffic scare on the way home, Henry admits that he loves her. A few months later, Henry helps Clare avenge herself on a boy who abused her and burned her with a cigarette during a date. Back in July 1995, twenty-four-year-old Clare and thirty-two-year-old Henry are in bed. Henry kisses her cigarette burn scar and Clare thanks him for helping her.

In 1988, when Clare is seventeen and Henry is thirty-six, she tells him that she notices how his moods often correspond to the time he has come from: "usually when you come from 1998, or '99 or 2000, you're upset or freaked out, and you won't tell me why. And then in 2001 you're okay again."

Chapter 6: Christmas Eve: One

On December 24, 1988, in the Reading Room, forty-year-old Henry remembers that it is the nineteenth anniversary of his mother's death. He knows his twenty-five-year-old self is observing the occasion by drinking himself sick. Henry reminisces about seeing his mother alive during his time travels and, for the first time, Henry tells seventeen-year-old Clare about his mother's fatal car accident. He was six, and though his mother was violently injured, he was unharmed. The stress and trauma of the moment had caused him to disappear from the car. He cannot bear Christmas because of these memories.

Chapter 7: Christmas Eve: Two

Twenty-five-year-old Henry is alone on Christmas Eve, 1988. He wanders around Chicago, wallowing in solitude and memories of his mother. He drinks himself into alcohol poisoning and wakes up hospitalized.

In April 1989, Clare is anxious about her separations from Henry, knowing a time is coming when she will not see him for two years. She and Grandma Meagram decide to take a walk in the Meadow, where they encounter forty-year-old Henry. Though blind, Grandma Meagram feels his presence. Eventually, Clare introduces them, but she lies about his age. When Henry disappears, Clare explains Henry's situation and their relationship.

Chapter 8: Eat or Be Eaten

In November 1991, twenty-eight-year-old Henry meets Clare's roommate Charisse Bonavant and Charisse's boyfriend, Jan Gomolinski (whom they call Gomez), at a dinner at Clare's apartment. When they are alone, Gomez warns twenty-year-old Clare about Henry without going into detail. He later tells Henry that he remembers seeing him around with Ingrid Carmichel. One month later, Gomez finds a thirty-six-year-old Henry, wearing a bizarre outfit, beating a man in an alley. Gomez accompanies Henry to a surplus store where Henry steals better clothing, then to a restaurant. Gomez says he knows about Henry's bad reputation and demands to know why things about Henry do not add up. Gomez says he knows Celia Attley and that Ingrid recently tried to kill herself. Henry tells him the truth, and he convinces Gomez he is a time traveler from the future when he disappears suddenly. The next day, Clare returns home from spending the night at Henry's apartment to find Gomez, who apologizes to her for misjudging Henry. He admits that Henry revealed his secret.

Clare is happy to have someone who understands, but Gomez asks her not to marry Henry in the future, believing he is too emotionally dangerous.

Thirty-three-year-old Henry arrives on December 22, 1991, at twenty-eight-year-old Henry's apartment. As the elder Henry promptly catches up on sleep, young Henry wonders why Clare finds this tense, tired man with short hair attractive. That same evening, Clare and the younger Henry attend the Violent Femmes concert. After Henry takes too long to return to their table with drinks, Clare finds him in an intimate, yet heated, argument with Ingrid, who Clare realizes must own the things she found in Henry's apartment after their first date. Ingrid's friend Celia tells Clare, "Henry, he's bad news, but he's Ingrid's bad news, and you be a fool to mess with him." Later, Clare is relieved to see the familiar Henry from the future. He asks Clare to be patient with the younger Henry, who needs her guidance, telling her, "It's a long way from the me you're dealing with in 1991 to me, talking to you right now from 1996."

Chapter 9: Christmas Eve, Three

Clare drives Henry to Meadowlark House to meet her family for Christmas 1991. During the trip, Henry offers his take on his time-traveling disorder: It occurs at times of stress or can be triggered by particular physical sensations like flashing light. He tries calming activities, such as running or sex, to stay in the present. He has no control over where or when he will appear, though he spends most of his time revisiting his past. At lunch with Clare's family, Henry wonders why her father and brother seem unnerved by him. That afternoon, Clare shows Henry the Meadow where his future self will appear to her, but she is disappointed when he does not recognize it.

After some family drama during Christmas dinner, Henry asks Clare why she did not share her family secrets with him before he came. Clare admits that she forgot he was the Henry who had not previously experienced these things. Clare's sister, Alicia, asks Clare if Henry has ever visited before. She remembers seeing a naked man in the Reading Room when she was twelve.

Late that evening when they attend church as a family, Helen and Ruth greet Henry and Clare. As Clare begins to introduce Henry, Helen tells her they have already met. Clare diffuses the situation, insisting Helen is wrong. The next evening, Clare takes Henry to a party at Laura's. Here, Helen interrogates Clare, demanding to know the real story about Henry. Clare tells her that she has known Henry since she was a child; they kept their relationship under wraps because of their age difference. The next morning Clare goes to say goodbye to Lucille and catches her mother writing a poem, which Lucille promptly hides, embarrassed. Clare leaves frustrated and disappointed in her dysfunctional family.

Chapter 10: Home is Where You Hang Your Head

Henry decides to go to his father's house in May 1992 to ask for his mother's wedding rings, but stops at Mrs. Kim's for advice. Kimy suggests he invite Clare and his dad to her place to make their first meeting more comfortable. Kimy also tells Henry that his father, Richard, has not paid his rent in two months, has not been working, and will not let her visit. Concerned, Henry lets himself into his father's apartment. His dad informs him that he can no longer play the violin because alcohol has damaged the nerves in his hands. Henry tells his dad he is marrying Clare and asks for the rings. When he tells his father that his mother would have liked Clare having the rings, Richard lashes out in grief and self-pity: "How would you know? You probably hardly remember her." Henry reveals that he has seen his mother in his time travels. Richard gives him the rings.

Chapter 11: Birthday

It is Clare's twenty-first birthday on May 24, 1992. When a twenty-eight-year-old Henry touches her intimately, she becomes edgy. She admits she feels physically overwhelmed by how often they have sex. Henry agrees to cool it, but he describes his perfect life as one with continuous sex and morning runs. When Clare asks why he enjoys running so much, Henry admits keeping in shape keeps him alive on his travels. He also tells her that his physical connection to her is what keeps him grounded in the present. Henry asks her to marry him. Clare says, "But you know, really … I already have." A month later, Clare meets Richard and

Kimy. The next month, Clare runs into Ingrid's friend, Celia, at a coffee shop. Celia has heard about their engagement and also seems to know about Henry's time traveling. She makes Clare come with her to a bar where Ingrid is waiting, and a scene erupts.

Chapter 12: Better Living Through Chemistry

Henry wants to find a drug to prevent him from disappearing at their wedding. Henry decides to visit Ben Matteson, chemist and friend with AIDS. He wants to take something that will keep him in the present for eight hours straight. Henry gives Ben a formula for a drug that will be available in a few years. Later, talking about possible consequences of the drugs with Clare, Henry flippantly remarks that he lives at least forty-three years. Later that month, Clare finds Henry on the kitchen floor of his apartment in a state that mimics Parkinson's disease. She calls 911 and Ben, who advises she stop his experiment with drugs. Henry is stabilized at the hospital.

Chapter 13: Turning Point

The day before the wedding, Henry goes into South Haven and gets his hair radically cut. In doing this, he has become his future self.

Chapter 14: Get Me to the Church on Time

On the day of his wedding, October 23, 1993, Henry hopes for a normal day. He runs along Maple

Street in the pouring rain, hoping to keep himself in the present. Later that morning, a thirty-eight-year-old Henry arrives and soon realizes it is his wedding day.

At the church later, Henry hears a noise outside and sees his future self giving him the OK sign. But when the wedding is ready to begin and Clare and her father knock on the groom's door, a future Henry answers wearing the younger Henry's tuxedo. The younger Henry returns and changes places with the older Henry after the ceremony. Charisse catches Clare's bouquet. Celia is among the guests, and Henry tells Ben that she is Ingrid's girlfriend. A few days later, present-day Henry and Clare get married at city hall.

Part Two: A Drop of Blood in a Bowl of Milk

Chapter 15: Married Life

Six months after their wedding, Clare has difficulty adjusting to marriage and their small two-bedroom flat. Though Clare craves her independence, she is frightened when Henry is away. He realizes their small apartment is cramping her inspiration and she needs a real studio. In April 1994, Henry gives Clare a winning lottery ticket worth $8 million, and at first, Clare feels the win is cheating, so Henry makes her a deal: They will not cash it in unless she wants to. But he thinks they should use it to buy a bigger studio—and other luxuries like a wedding present for Charisse and Gomez.

A month after their winning, Clare and Henry look for a house. He informs Clare that he has briefly visited their future home and knows what the backyard is supposed to look like. Later that year, Clare, Henry, Gomez, and Charisse hang out at Lighthouse Beach and a bookstore called Bookman's Alley. At the book shop, Henry notices Gomez gazing at Clare with longing.

In February 1995, Henry and Clare are spending the evening with Charisse and Gomez when they hear a tremendous crash in the kitchen. They find a future Henry there, bloody with a head injury after landing on a wood and glass cabinet. The injured Henry demands a drink and swallows a good amount of whiskey before disappearing violently, leaving them all shaken.

Chapter 16: Library Science Fiction

The next month, Matt, one of Henry's co-workers, catches Henry naked in the stacks at the Newberry, not for the first time. Henry fears one day getting trapped in the "cage," four stories tall, made of beige steel, and located in the center of one of the Newberry stairwells. If he ever gets trapped inside the cage, he will not be able to escape unless he disappears.

On March 11, 1996, Dr. Kendrick meets Henry for the first time, but he does not believe Henry's story of Chrono-Impairment. Henry gives the doctor information about Dr. Kendrick's unborn child. Dr. Kendrick scoffs; he is supposed to have a daughter, not a son. In addition, Henry predicts the son will be born with Down Syndrome. A month later, Dr. Kendrick is stunned that Henry's predictions were correct. Henry meets with Kendrick and explains everything. At first, Kendrick does not see any downside to Henry's situation, particularly having information about the future. He agrees to help after he sees Henry disappear and dangerously reappear.

Chapter 17: A Very Small Shoe

In the spring of 1996, after two years of marriage, Henry and Clare decide to have a child. She is obsessed, wanting a child so she can always hold onto a part of Henry when he leaves. Henry thinks about having a normal child with Clare, one that will not inherit his time-travel genes. He knows a baby would ease Clare's anxiety when he comes and goes, but he worries that his child would be just like him.

Chapter 18: One

Clare is eight weeks pregnant in June 1996. Clare starts bleeding when Henry is away, so Charisse and Gomez take her to the hospital, where she loses the child.

In a sleep lab, Henry has nightmares that belie his anxiety. In his last dream, he is in the snow, bloody and naked. He wakes up in the lab bleeding, much to Kendrick's excitement.

Chapter 19: Two

Clare miscarries her second pregnancy on October 12, 1997, in bed overnight.

Early in 1998, Kendrick tells Henry that he is going to test a genetic therapy on mice, hoping to understand Henry's condition.

Chapter 20: Intermezzo

Clare's mother dies in August 1998 of ovarian cancer. Clare is devastated. In November, Clare decides to go through her mother's desk and put her papers in order. She asks Henry to pick the lock. She finds a poem dedicated to her: "The Garden Under the Snow, for Clare." Henry finds Clare crying with joy over the words her mother wrote for her.

Chapter 21: New Year's Eve, One

In 1999, Henry and Clare celebrate New Year's Eve with Charisse and Gomez on a rooftop in Wicker Park. Henry reminisces about things he knows about Chicago's future and, as midnight comes and goes, wishes that time would stand still for him and Clare.

Chapter 22: Three

In March 1999, Henry and Clare visit Charisse and Gomez to see their third child. Though Henry is happy for his friends, he can only feel sorry about the three pregnancies he and Clare lost. Gomez tells Henry about a friend, Dr. Amit Montague, who specializes in fetal chromosome disorders and might be able to help.

Chapter 23: Four

After losing a fourth child in July 1999, Henry and Clare are both on edge. Henry leaves the house during one of their confrontations, too exhausted to deal with the issue any longer. He has asked future selves if he and Clare will have a child, but his future selves answer cryptically. Henry goes to a pier to think and vanishes. Clare watches the police, firemen, and television news crews surround the pier where Henry disappeared. A policeman apparently saw him jump and grills Clare about whether Henry regularly swims at night or if they had an argument. Henry appears, naked and cold. He tells the police he was wearing earplugs and did not hear them calling.

In 2000, Kendrick shows Clare and Henry a time-traveling mouse that vanishes in his cage and reappears in a lab in the basement. Kendrick has cloned Henry's DNA and inserted it into mice embryos. He tells Henry and Clare that the most difficult part is getting the babies carried to term. Both mother mouse and baby keep dying because the embryo travels outside the womb and back, causing the mother to bleed internally. Kendrick tells them how he solved the problem. Henry and Clare are encouraged.

Chapter 24: Five

A fifth child has been lost by May 2000. Clare

tells a future Henry she is ready to give up, but he tells her that in his time, they have a child. He also tells her his present self is trying to prevent them from getting pregnant, and that the present Henry does not know that children are in their future. Clare will have to be quiet about what she knows, whatever happens.

Chapter 25: Six

A month later, Clare finds condoms in their grocery bags and confronts Henry. He tells her five miscarriages are enough and he does not want her to die with the next one. Clare prays to her future child, urging it to arrive soon. Following Clare's fifth miscarriage, Henry decides to get a vasectomy without Clare knowing. Sick with anxiety, Henry vanishes into the Meadow where Clare is fifteen. Clare greets him, but he tries to avoid her. Clare demands to know what is going on. When he says nothing, she hits him. She asks again, and he refuses to say. She bites him hard, and he still refuses to answer but kisses her roughly. It is their first kiss.

When he returns to 2000, Henry asks Clare if she remembers the first time they kissed. He apologizes for the violence. She asks why he was upset that day. He will not say. She says she knows he went to get a vasectomy because she saw the imprint of the appointment on a notepad. She tells him to go ahead with the surgery. They make love. Four weeks later, she discovers she is pregnant for the sixth time.

Chapter 26: Baby Dreams

During her pregnancy, Clare has disturbing dreams that reflect her worry about having a healthy child. She feels like she and the baby are desperately trying to survive. Dr. Montague and Henry try to reassure her. On September 27, 2000, Clare miscarries while Henry is not there.

Chapter 27: Seven

A Henry from the past makes love to Clare in December 2000. She becomes pregnant with their seventh child. Less than two months later, Clare tells Henry she is pregnant. At first, Henry is confused, but suddenly remembers the unusual circumstances. Two months later, Dr. Montague shows them their healthy baby in an ultrasound. In August, Clare and Henry choose a name for the baby: Alba DeTamble.

Chapter 28: Alba, An Introduction

Henry arrives at the Art Institute in Chicago in 2011, despite the fact Alba will be born at any moment. After idly watching a group of school children on a field trip, he realizes one particularly inquisitive girl is his daughter. Alba sees Henry in the gallery and recognizes him. Her teacher is stunned because her father is dead. Alba tries to explain that Henry is not completely dead by telling her teacher that he is a CDP. After a phone call to Clare, the teacher allows the reunion. Clare tells Henry and Alba she will join them at the museum as soon as she can. While they wait for Clare to arrive,

Alba explains the meaning of CDP to Henry: Chrono-Displaced Person. It is the first time Henry has met his daughter, because for him she is not yet born. Alba tells him she is learning to play the violin from his father. She also tells him that she has seen Henry's mother in the past. Henry learns that Alba can go wherever and whenever she wants, and he tells her to visit him. She actually has visited, one night when he was with Ingrid. Henry returns to 2001 and tells Clare he visited the future and saw their daughter, ten years old and a CDP like him.

Chapter 29: Birthday

Alba is born on September 5, 2001. Later, Henry's father visits his granddaughter in the hospital. Henry says Alba will be a violinist and Richard will be her teacher. Feeding the baby early one morning, they see coverage of 9/11 on television. When Alba is ten months old, Clare sketches her to record her life and to commemorate Clare's and Henry's love for her.

Chapter 30: Secret

Clare revels being alone without Henry. She can listen to whatever music she likes, hang out with her friends (including Celia), and ride her bike. But though she enjoys her independence, she always longs for him to return.

Chapter 31: Experiencing Technical Difficulties

Clare has a successful show in May 2004 at the

Chicago Cultural Center: an exhibit of wire and paper birds. While Henry is holding Alba, he realizes he is going to disappear. He pushes Alba toward Richard and vanishes.

Chapter 32: Nature Morte

The next month, Henry reappears, gaunt, filthy, and badly hurt. Out shopping, Clare and Alba run into Kendrick and his family. Clare tells Kendrick that Henry has been time traveling frequently, which the doctor did not know. Kendrick asks Clare why she will not let him test Alba's DNA. Clare emphatically says she will not risk Alba's life.

Chapter 33: Birthday

It is Clare's eighteenth birthday. Henry arrives at the Meadow on May 24, 1989, to find Clare waiting for him with a tuxedo and a romantic picnic for two. Henry apologizes for not bringing a gift, but Clare reminds him of a pact they had made last time they saw each other. Since it is Clare's eighteenth birthday and this would be the last day they would see each other for two years, they would make love. Henry is nervous, but he promises to be gentle. Afterward, Clare asks him when they will meet again and where. Henry does not want to tell her; he wants everything to unfold they way it is supposed to. He does say that when she sees him next, he will not know her.

Chapter 34: Secret

Henry arrives in 2005 from the day they made love and chides Clare for not telling him about the first time they made love. Clare admits she went through a bout of depression during the two years they did not see each other, but her parents forced her into therapy and eventually she went back to a normal life. She thinks about the one drunken night in 1990 she slept with Gomez, and after some anxiety eventually tells Henry, who understands.

Clare recalls the time she slept with Gomez in April 1990. Guilty about hurting both Charisse and Henry, Clare tells Gomez that Henry is her lover. She shows Gomez a photo of Henry and he tells her he has seen Henry before. Twenty-six-year-old Henry is with Ingrid at the Iggy Pop concert in April 1990 and runs into Gomez. Gomez, whom he does not know at this point, tells him Clare says hello. Henry does not know who he is talking about and goes home with Ingrid.

Henry takes Charisse to the opera in 2005 because neither Clare nor Gomez would enjoy it. After the opera, Henry and Charisse discuss Gomez's lifelong crush on Clare. Charisse tells Henry that Gomez is waiting for Henry to disappear for good. She asks Henry if Gomez ever leaves her. Henry says no.

Early in 2006, Clare sees little Alba playing with an older Alba in the backyard. Little Alba introduces older Alba to Clare. Elder Alba is thrilled to see her daddy alive, but Henry tells elder Alba not to mention his death to her mother or little Alba. They all spend a nice afternoon as a family before elder Alba disappears.

Chapter 35: The Episode of the Monroe Street Parking Garage

On January 7, 2006, Henry answers the phone in the middle of the night. His future self needs help at the Monroe Street Parking Garage. Clare and Henry go to meet him but he is no longer there. They both know something is very wrong.

Chapter 36: Birthday

For Henry's birthday, June 16, 2006, Clare buys a recording of his mother performing in an opera. The next day, Henry and Clare go to the Brookfield Zoo with Gomez and Charisse and their kids. That evening, Clare has arranged for a babysitter while they have dinner, prepared by her childhood family cook Nell and served by her art school friend Lourdes. Clare gives Henry his mother's recording. It is the perfect evening. As they drift off to sleep, Clare says, "I feel like we're at the top of a roller coaster."

Chapter 37: An Unpleasant Scene

In June 2006, a forty-three-year-old Henry appears in the future inside the cage at the Newberry. He is caught by security guards Kevin and Roy, who summon Matt and Roberto. At the same moment, present-day Henry walks into his office and sees Matt, who just returned from checking on the caged Henry. He explains his condition to Roberto, detailing Kendrick's research.

Roberto does not fire him. The rest of his co-workers compare him to Clark Kent and Superman.

The next month, Kendrick tells Henry that the experimental therapy he has been working on with mice will not work on Henry because of his age and his poor immune system. Henry asks if it will work with Alba. Kendrick tells him that Clare will not let him work with Alba. Henry decides to get some of Alba's DNA so Kendrick can test her. When Alba turns eighteen, she can decide whether to use the formula or not.

Henry thinks about his death. He is in the Meadow on October 27, 1984, wearing the black clothes thirteen-year-old Clare packed for him. Philip and Mark are hunting deer. They see a clumsy large flash of something appear in the field near Henry, whom they do not see. They shoot, and Henry hears a scream. Another Henry has appeared from another time stumbling through the meadow. That future Henry is shot. Henry motions for Clare not to be alarmed. But the wounded Henry has vanished somewhere to die.

Chapter 38: The Episode of the Monroe Street Parking Garage

The wounded Henry has arrived in January 2006 and is freezing. He cannot feel his feet. He crawls to the parking garage, where he calls Clare and his younger self. They rush to help him, but he vanishes before they arrive.

Chapter 39: Fragments

Present-day Henry has been gone for the day when he crashes into the living room on September 25, 2006, with frostbite. Clare calls an ambulance. Later, doctors treat Henry for frostbite but the prognosis does not look good. The following night Henry's feet are amputated above the ankles.

In October, Henry is home from the hospital. He has no appetite. He does not speak with Clare. Alba says the future Alba told her that he was dying, but he denies it. He is depressed and short-tempered toward both Clare and Alba. Clare begins to make paper and construct wings. Kimy visits Henry and helps him stop feeling sorry for himself briefly. Clare continues work on the wings, and a week later, shows Henry. They kiss.

Chapter 40: Feet Dreams

Henry dreams about losing his feet, about feet that no longer work, and about feet that break and hurt. A month later, feeling better, Henry teaches Alba and Clare how to cook, to prepare them for when he is no longer around.

Chapter 41: What Goes Around Comes Around

Henry appears on the floor of Ingrid's apartment in January 1994. He is in so much pain that he cannot muster tact; he shows her his legs and she offers him opiate-based painkillers. He realizes that he has appeared on the day she will commit suicide. She asks what will become of her, and he tries to assure her that her life goes on. He tries to stop her, but she pulls a gun and shoots herself in the chest.

Henry arrives back home in December 2006 and tells Clare about Ingrid. He wishes he could have stopped her. He tells Clare that when he dies she should look in his desk, where he has organized important papers.

Chapter 42: Hours, If Not Days

On Christmas Eve, Henry knows it will not be long before his death. He tries to enjoy the remaining time with Alba and Clare.

Chapter 43: New Year's Eve, Two

Henry and Clare have a New Year's party and invite all their close family and friends. Celia gives Henry a photo of himself, from the younger days when he dated Ingrid. Henry tells Gomez how much their relationship has meant to him and that he will die soon. In another room, Ben speaks to Clare about Henry. He is worried about Henry's depression. Ben thinks Henry is about to die. Clare finds Henry, who tells her it is time. They kiss, but as the clock strikes midnight, he vanishes.

Part Three: A Treatise on Longing

Henry knows what comes next. He jumps to October 27, 1984, and right back to the party on January 1, 2007, dying from a gunshot.

In 2007, Clare tries to go on without Henry,

but she cannot sleep or eat. Kimy helps her take care of Alba. Clare reads a letter Henry left to be opened after his death. He tells her not to wait for him and to live the rest of her life to the fullest. He also tells her that he has seen her as an old woman.

Gomez visits Clare in July 2008 to see how she is doing. Weary with grief, she turns to Gomez for comfort and makes love to him. A few weeks later, in front of Charisse, Alba asks Clare when Henry is coming home. She explains to Charisse that Alba and Henry visit each other.

Henry and Ingrid are out on a date in 1990 when they encounter Alba. Henry does not know who Alba is, but she gives him a quick kiss. Father and daughter meet in 1979, when Henry is forty-two and Alba is ten. He begins to tell her a story saying, "Once upon a time—" She interrupts to correct him: "All times at once. A long time ago, and right now."

At last, in 2053, when Henry is forty-three and Clare is eighty-two, they are reunited.

Alicia Abshire

Alicia is Clare's sister. She is three years younger than Clare. Alicia is a talented cellist who searches for acceptance from her parents, yet rebels against them. After meeting Henry when Clare brings him home to Meadowlark House, she tells Clare about seeing someone who looked like him when she was younger and mistaking him for a prowler.

Lucille Abshire

Lucille is Clare's mother. She does not approve of Mark and Sharon's engagement because of Sharon's pregnancy, despite the fact that her marriage came about the same way. She suffers from bipolar disorder. She dies of ovarian cancer.

Mark Abshire

Mark is Clare's older brother. Mark studied pre-law at Harvard and is engaged to Sharon, who is pregnant with his child. Mark is present at the hunting accident that kills Henry.

Philip Abshire

Philip is Clare's father, a balding middle-aged lawyer who specializes in wills and trusts and enjoys hunting. He is hunting with Mark when Henry is accidentally shot.

Celia Attley

Celia is a small woman with long dreadlocks who comes into the drama attached to Ingrid. Celia confronts Clare when Clare begins dating Henry. Celia warns Clare not to get involved with Henry because he is already involved with Ingrid, the woman Celia loves. Despite her connection with Ingrid, Celia becomes good friends with Clare and attends Henry's and Clare's wedding.

Charisse Bonavant

Charisse is Clare's best friend and roommate from 1991. She marries Gomez and they have three children, yet Charisse worries about his lingering crush on Clare. Called a "Filipino Madonna" by Henry, she is an easy-going and no-nonsense character.

Roberto Calle

Roberto is Henry's boss at the Newberry Library. He specializes in the Italian Renaissance and is the head of Special Collections. Roberto catches Henry in compromising situations, particularly when Henry appears in the cage, but he is supportive and encouraging. He does not fire

Henry despite Henry's odd and unpredictable behavior at work.

Media Adaptations

- An unabridged audio recording of *The Time Traveler's Wife* was released by Highbridge Audio in 2006. It is available on compact disc.

Ingrid Carmichel

Ingrid is Henry's girlfriend before he meets Clare. Ingrid is desperate for Henry's love and affection. She becomes furious when Henry leaves her for Clare and eventually grows suicidal. Henry tries to talk Ingrid out of killing herself, but she shoots herself in his presence.

Alba DeTamble

Alba is Henry and Clare's daughter. She has Chrono-Impairment like her father, but she is able to control the condition better than he can. She is stoic, intelligent, and adventurous. She thinks time traveling is interesting.

Clare Abshire DeTamble

Clare is the woman at the center of the novel, which chronicles her unusual relationship with Henry DeTamble from the moment she meets him as a child to their reunion when she is an old woman. Though Clare's personality and personal interests change with age, the heart of her identity is defined by her experiences with, and love for, Henry. Her life's path is shaped by Henry's presence or absence; when he vanishes, she is constantly waiting for him to return. An artist who works with paper, Clare comes from a wealthy family, with an older brother Mark and a younger sister Alicia. She is an inquisitive child, a pragmatic adult, and a bad cook.

Henry DeTamble

The novel follows Henry's experiences with Chrono-Impairment, a condition that causes him to time travel uncontrollably, and how those experiences affect his relationship with Clare. He first travels as a child after a visit to the Field Museum of Natural History and soon learns from his older self how to survive by stealing money and clothing. As a young man, Henry deals with the emotions brought on by the unexpected traveling through drinking, partying, and sleeping around. As he ages, Henry longs to become normal and fears losing everyone he loves, particularly Clare. Though he confides in Kimy, Clare is the only person who grounds him in reality, yet her love cannot keep him in one place for long. Henry is the son of a violinist for the Chicago Symphony Orchestra and a famous opera singer, Annette Lyn Robinson, who dies in a gruesome car accident. Henry believes he should have died in the accident along with his mother, but instead the stress caused him to time travel from the car to safety. Henry constantly refers to a wide variety of literature, which reflects his literature studies in college, and he learned to speak German and French as a child when his mother toured the world.

Richard DeTamble

Richard DeTamble is Henry's father. A violinist with the Chicago Symphony, Richard slowly destroys his career and the nerves in his hands with chronic alcoholism. Depressed and racked with guilt over his wife's death, he isolates himself from friends and family. Richard begins to heal when Henry tells Richard about his engagement to Clare and later rediscovers his purpose in life when Henry informs him that he will teach Henry and Clare's daughter Alba how to play the violin.

Dulcie

Great Aunt Dulcie is Clare's great aunt. She reminds Lucille at Christmas dinner that Lucille is a hypocrite for disliking Sharon because of her pregnancy because Lucille was in the same situation once herself.

Jason Everleigh

Clare dates Jason, a football player, when she is sixteen. Jason physically abuses her, and as punishment, Clare asks Henry to help punish Jason by tying him to a tree and recording the details of the abuse on his body with a marker. She then invites all the girls in their school to look at him.

Gomez

"Gomez" is the nickname of Jan Gomolinski. He enters the story as the boyfriend of Charisse, Clare's roommate, whom he later marries. He warns Clare about Henry's bad reputation when they first meet, but he and Charisse become Clare and Henry's best friends and confidantes about Henry's condition. Gomez has a longstanding crush on Clare.

Rosa Evangeline Gomolinski

Rosa is Gomez and Charisse's third child. She reminds Henry of the children he and Clare have lost.

Jan Gomolinski

See Gomez.

Joseph Gomolinski

Joseph is Gomez and Charisse's second child.

Maximilian Gomolinski

Max is Gomez and Charisse's first child.

David Kendrick

A geneticist and a philosopher, Dr. Kendrick uses mice injected with Henry's DNA to help him devise a treatment plan for Henry. His research leads Henry and Clare to realize why Clare has not been able to carry a child to term. Dr. Kendrick is married with two children.

Colin Kendrick

Colin is Dr. Kendrick's son, who has Down Syndrome. Dr. Kendrick and his wife are stunned when Henry predicts their son's condition before he is born, particularly because they are expecting a healthy daughter.

Kevin

Henry calls Kevin the "Security Nazi" at the Newberry Library. Kevin is the first person to find

Henry in the cage at the library.

Kim

Mr. Kim is the gruff landlord of the building where Henry grows up.

Kim

See Kimy.

Kimy

Kimy is Mr. Kim's widow and the landlady of the building where Henry grew up. Kimy has been Henry's confidante since childhood. She is an excellent cook and acts as Henry's surrogate mother over the years.

Matt

Matt is one of Henry's co-workers at the Newberry Library. He frequently finds Henry naked in the stacks and is the first person to see two Henrys when both show up in the same time period.

Ben Matteson

Ben is Henry's friend. A chemist with AIDS, Ben helps Henry cope with his time traveling by creating a drug to try to help Henry.

Meagram

Grandma Meagram is Clare's maternal grandmother. She is nearly blind, and she meets Henry shortly before she dies. She is the only person Clare tells about Henry before they meet in what is "present-day" Chicago for both of them.

Etta Milbauer

Etta acts as a mother figure for Clare throughout her childhood. She is the housekeeper at Meadowlark House.

Amit Montague

Dr. Montague, a fetal chromosome specialist, is recommended to Henry and Clare by Gomez to help them carry a child to term. She is French Moroccan, calm, competent, and elegant. She delivers their daughter, Alba.

Murray

Dr. Murray helps try to save Henry's legs and feet after frostbite. She is imposing and confident.

Nell

Nell is the cook at the Meadowlark House whom Clare describes as "Aretha Franklin meets Julia Child." At Clare's request, she helps one of Clare's art school friends create a lovely birthday dinner for Henry.

Nick

Henry beats up Nick, a "homophobic yuppie," after Nick initiates a fight because of Henry's odd wardrobe. Gomez went to law school with Nick and catches Henry in the middle of the beating.

Helen Powell

A childhood friend of Clare's, Helen suspects Henry is Clare's boyfriend, despite the vast age difference.

Annette Lyn Robinson

A famous opera singer with no culinary skills, Annette is Henry's flamboyant mother. The memory of her violent death haunts Henry throughout the novel; she was decapitated during a car crash when Henry was six.

Roy

Henry calls Roy the "King of the Main Desk" at the Newberry Library. Roy has a good disposition and a wonderful smile. Kevin calls Roy when he finds Henry in the cage at the library. Roy brings the trapped Henry coffee.

Sharon

Sharon is Mark's pregnant fiancée. Her parents are upset about her pregnancy because she might not continue with her plans to attend medical school. She comes from a Catholic family in Jacksonville, Florida, and does not like cold weather.

Themes

Love Conquers All

Though *The Time Traveler's Wife* works on a science fiction level, the novel is a love story at heart. Henry and Clare are lovers who miss each other in time and space, but they are meant to be together against all odds. From the desperate yearnings and impossible obstacles of Henry and Clare to the framing of the novel with Derek Walcott's poem, "Love After Love," at its open and an excerpt from Homer's *Odyssey* at its close, *The Time Traveler's Wife* undeniably offers the message that love can survive and is eternal.

Cataloguing the Past

In *The Time Traveler's Wife*, certain places and objects emphasize Henry's and Clare's need to keep the past, present, and future in order. Both the Field Museum of Natural History and the Newberry Library are places where the past and present are archived for future generations. At the museum, fossils and bones are neatly displayed to record life in another time. At the library, ancient manuscripts are restored and shown in the same manner. Essentially, libraries and museums strive to resurrect the past and keep it alive in the present and future. This acts as a direct parallel to Henry's ability to exist in many times at once, as well as his need to prevent his life from being forgotten.

In a personal context, Clare keeps a diary and makes sketches as testimony to her past experiences and proof of her encounters with Henry. Like the Field Museum and the Newberry Library, the diary keeps the past alive by documenting memories and offering tangible evidence that they actually occurred.

Defining Right and Wrong

The Time Traveler's Wife inspires much discussion about morality and ethics. For example, Henry teaches his younger self how to steal to survive the time travel experience. But does one person's survival justify another person's loss? In terms of Henry and Clare's relationship, Henry and Clare marry as adults, but they begin their close relationship when Henry is a grown man and Clare is a child. Although they do not consummate their relationship until Clare is eighteen, Henry finds himself drawn to the young Clare. The difference in their ages throughout the story poses complex questions about the right age for certain experiences, particularly sexual relationships. Dr. Kendrick's involvement with Henry's DNA echoes the complicated and controversial issues that surround cloning: Should one tamper with nature? Does experimenting with DNA challenge religious beliefs?

Style

Point of View

The Time Traveler's Wife shifts between two narrators: Henry and Clare. The frequent change in point of view is clearly indicated by a header. Each narrative is written in first-person, and although Henry and Clare have distinctive voices, the headers keep the reader fully aware of who is telling the story.

The dual point-of-view approach emphasizes the parallel timelines, as well as allows the reader to understand both the complexities and effects of Henry's condition. Without insight into both Henry's and Clare's points of view, the reader would not fully experience the emotional intensity of the story. The two distinct narratives also highlight the distance and time ever present between Henry and Clare and allow the reader to sympathize with both.

Topics for Further Study

- Study the poems by Derek Walcott, Rainer Maria Rilke, and A. S. Byatt that frame the major sections of *The Time Traveler's Wife*. Write an essay on how these poems reflect the themes of the novel and show the character development of protagonists Clare and Henry.

- In *The Time Traveler's Wife*, Clare begins her relationship with Henry when she is six and he is thirty-six. Though they marry when both are adults, their unusual story introduces complex moral issues. With your classmates or friends, discuss Henry's and Clare's complicated relationship, and then write an essay that sums up your personal perspective. Do you think Henry is influencing Clare's future by shaping her young and immature feelings? Does the fact that they eventually marry negate their age difference in the early stages of their relationship? What if Henry was not a time traveler? How would that change the meaning of the love story?

- When they first meet, Henry and Clare spend time discussing free will and determinism, or fate, and God. As narrator, Henry tells the reader that over time Clare will change her mind about what she believes. In an essay, explore the evolution of Clare's beliefs throughout the novel, using examples from the book.

- The elder Henry tries not to tell Clare or his past self about future events. Why was keeping those secrets important to Henry? If you could time travel like Henry, would you tell your past self about the future? Are there any past events you would change? Do you think you would have the power to change them? Discuss your opinions in a small group.

Time

The title of each "chapter" of *The Time Traveler's Wife* marks a particular event or experience for Henry or Clare, and each chapter is divided with specific time stamps. These precise dates and times are as important to the reader as to Henry and Clare. The reader and the protagonists must fit pieces of time together like clues in a mystery to understand and experience the story being told. Henry's travels in time also mark turning points in the story. Logistically, three timelines work to keep this story coherent: Clare's timeline, Henry's timeline, and a universal timeline. These three co-exist, forcing the reader to participate in the story by keeping times and dates straight.

Motifs

Niffenegger uses sex throughout *The Time Traveler's Wife* as more than a natural physical experience. For Henry, having sexual encounters provides a way to stay connected to a time and place. As a young man in his early twenties, Henry is known for his sexual exploits with women. Niffenegger uses the experiences to show Henry's desperation for human connection and physical contact. In addition, activities such as running and making love prevent Henry from disappearing into another time. Clare once complains to Henry about their intense sexual relationship. Henry uses sex literally to hold onto Clare. Niffenegger complicates sexual issues with ethical questions by constantly addressing the age difference between Henry and Clare, particularly through references to Vladimir Nabokov's classic, *Lolita*.

Children are another motif in *The Time Traveler's Wife*. Clare meets Henry when she is a child, Henry discovers his time-traveling power when he is a child, and they are finally connected in time through their child, Alba. Throughout the novel, children represent the markers of time, illustrating how people grow and mature. They represent hope for the future and a way to allow love to live beyond death. For Clare and Henry, Alba is both a tangible symbol of their love and evidence that they were once together.

Historical Context

Chicago

To ground the fantastical elements of *The Time Traveler's Wife*, Niffenegger paints a vivid picture of Chicago and its main attractions. Early in the novel, an older Henry visits his younger self at the Field Museum of Natural History. Founded in 1893, the museum once was known as the Chicago Natural History Museum and is located on Chicago's famous Lake Shore Drive.

As the story progresses, Clare creates and shows her work at the Art Institute of Chicago. The Institute, both a museum and a school, was constructed in 1879 from the rubble left after the 1871 Great Chicago Fire. Henry's mother, Annette Lyn Robinson, sings for the Lyric Opera, housed in Chicago's famous Civic Opera House with its elegant Art Deco-style interior. Niffenegger provides another notable locale when Henry and Gomez eat at Ann Sather's Swedish Restaurant, established in 1945 on Belmont Avenue. Another unmistakable Chicago symbol since the turn of the century is the El Train, or Elevated Train, which Henry rides across town late at night.

Punk Music

The Punk Rock Movement began in London

during the 1970s, but it quickly traveled abroad to develop an American style in New York City. Punk rockers rebelled against everything: society, government, religion, and even their own identities. Their music reflected this intense feeling of alienation as well as the rockers' gravitation toward anarchy and their rejection of rules, conformity, and order. Some popular bands mentioned in *The Time Traveler's Wife*: Iggy Pop, the Violent Femmes, and The Shags. Both Henry and Clare enjoy this type of music; punk reflects their feelings of alienation throughout the novel, not to mention their yearning to make sense of Henry's chaotic condition.

Critical Overview

For a first novel, *The Time Traveler's Wife* received tremendous accolades. In its review of an audio version, *Publisher's Weekly* called it a "clever and inventive tale which works on three levels: as an intriguing science fiction concept, a realistic character study and a touching love story." *Library Journal* deemed the novel "skillfully written with a blend of distinct characters and heartfelt emotions that hopscotch through time, begging interpretation on many levels." Elsa Gaztambide of *BookList* called it a "hip and urban love story." Liz Fraser of New Zealand's *book-club.com* praised it as "an unashamed sentimental tear jerker," admitting, "If I was more cynical I could suggest that the book is overly sentimental."

While most critics enjoyed the overall effort, some found fault with the author's debut novel. In the *Boston Globe*, Judith Mass noted, "Apart from their time-travel difficulties, Henry and Clare are not particularly compelling." Eric Weinberger of the *Washington Post* qualified his praise for Niffenegger's novel, writing, "her narrative method suffers from a surplus of self-consciousness." Even in these less-than-glowing reviews, the critics still endorsed the book.

The Time Traveler's Wife was nominated for several awards, from the Orange Prize for Fiction to the Arthur C. Clarke Award. The novel won a 2003

Listen Up Award, a 2004 Alex Award, and a 2006 British Book Award.

What Do I Read Next?

- Charles Dickinson's *A Shortcut in Time* (2003) follows Euclid, Illinois, resident Josh Winkler, a local artist, as he takes a shortcut down a familiar path and ends up fifteen minutes in the past. A woman appears from the turn of the century, suddenly making Josh's life even more complicated.

- Keith Donohue's *The Stolen Child* (2006) tells the magical tale of a boy and his changeling—a faery being who replaces him in the world when he is kidnapped at the age of seven. The story alternates between the point of view of the human, living among the faeries and never aging, and his replacement, who grows up and goes on with life in the world. Both yearn to return to their rightful places.

- Diana Gabaldon's *A Breath of Snow and Ashes* (2005), set during the American Revolution, is the sixth novel in Gabaldon's bestselling *Outlander* saga. It continues the romantic time-traveling adventures of eighteenth-century Scotsman Jamie Fraser and his twentieth-century wife, Claire.

- *The Three Incestuous Sisters: An Illustrated Novel* (2005) is Niffeneger's follow-up to *The Time Traveler's Wife*. The 176-page book features an aquatint etching on every other page, accompanied by only a few lines of text. Like *The Time Traveler's Wife*, it is based on a fantastical premise and addresses the connectedness of people who love each other.

- Derek Walcott's *Collected Poems: 1948–1984* (1987) provides a broad selection of the Nobel laureate's work. The Caribbean-born poet is noted for his style of magical realism. His poem "Love After Love" appears opposite

Niffenegger's dedication to her grandparents in the first pages of *The Time Traveler's Wife*.

Sources

"Author Audrey Neffenegger's Biography," in *Book Browse*, www.bookbrowse.com/biographies/index.cfm?author_number=928 (June 29, 2006).

"Between the Lines: An Interview with Audrey Niffenegger," www.harcourtbooks.com/authorinterviews/bookinter (July 15, 2006).

Billen, Andrew, "Success Was All a Matter of Time," in the *Times (London)*, March 28, 2006, p. 8.

Fraser, Liz, Review of *The Time Traveler's Wife*, on book-club.co.nz (July 21, 2006).

Gaztambide, Elsa, Review of *The Time Traveler's Wife*, in *BookList*, September 1, 2003, p. 59.

Mass, Judith, "An Uneven Chronicle of a Couple over Time," in the *Boston Globe*, December 8, 2003, bostonglobe.com (July 21, 2006).

Review of Highbridge Audio version of *The Time Traveler's Wife*, in *Publisher's Weekly*, December 1, 2003, p. 20.

Review of *The Time Traveler's Wife*, in the *Library Journal*, Vol. 28, No. 13, August 15, 2003, p. 134.

Weinberger, Eric, Review of *The Time Traveler's Wife*, in the *Washington Post*, November 3, 2003, washingtonpost.com (July 21, 2006).

Further Reading

Nabokov, Vladimir, *Lolita*, Random House, 1955.

> In *Lolita*, Humbert Humbert, an older man, develops an unusual and intense relationship with a twelve-year-old girl, generating moral and ethical questions about sexuality and age.

Rilke, Rainer Maria, *The Selected Poetry of Rainer Maria Rilke*, Vintage, 1989.

> The book is a volume of English translations of Rilke's German poetry about life, love, and beauty. An excerpt from his *The Ninth Duino Elegy* is excerpted in *The Time Traveler's Wife*.

Schulze, Franz, and Kevin Harrington, *Chicago's Famous Buildings*, University of Chicago Press, 2003.

> The fifth edition of *Chicago's Famous Buildings* illustrates recent architectural additions to the city, as well as the city's classic structures. The book also addresses future development of Chicago's diverse neighborhoods and provides current maps as a walking guide.

Lightning Source UK Ltd.
Milton Keynes UK
UKHW021123041122
411640UK00009B/180